The Words That Heal

Encouragement for the Soul

Stacie P. Thompson

Scripture taken from the New King James Version®. Copyright © 1982 by Thomas Nelson.

Used by permission. All rights reserved

Copyright 2015,

Anointed Ink Publishing

PO Box 1424

Highland, NY 12528

ISBN: 978- 0692488928

Control: 2015946428

This book is dedicated to my friend Alecia Johnson:

My friend, my inspiration, my motivation!

Alecia, I have watched you stand in the face of adversity with Power, Strength and Confidence. You define courage! In the midst of your trials you managed to encourage, motivate and push me to attain my goals. I love you Suga!

Thank you!

Foreword

Life has the ability to develop for one experiences and hope. If your experiences destroy your hope, then without hope, you ultimately have no life. In *The Words That Heal Encouragement for the Soul,* Sis. Stacie Thompson, demonstrates the results of standing in the optimistic perception developed through a hope, formed from the foundation(s) of prayers, inspirations, and those who have served as examples in her life.

The Bible tells us that if any man be in Christ, he is a new creature. Old things are passed away and [behold] all things are become new. Your life, at this very moment, is in one of two places. You are *becoming* or *have become.* The hope that's demonstrated here is to be in a place of knowing that something good is about to happen to you. As long as you develop strategic behaviors based on the instructions and revelations of the word, your steps will surely be ordered correctly.

This writing of the heart is sure to be one that is not a one-time read, but it speaks to the heart of matters that will undoubtedly happen in your life time and time again. Each time you revisit the writings of Thompson, you will gain more strength in the face of weakening situations. It's a blessing to know that you are not facing your next situation alone, but you now have a roadmap to develop the right responses in the right situations. There is detailed inspiration within these covers to give you the answers you need for survival and victory!

With great joy, I excitedly endorse any and all individuals to learn as much as you can from this genuine mother, believer, and now published author!

Pastor Lenny Gaines

PowerHouse Christian Church, Pendleton SC

God's Purpose for Me...

"Stacie, I have created you to be a living example to other women, an example of strength through adversity, heartache, disappointment and lack.

You are here to tell others how you deal with "friends" who smile in your face; talk about you and try to tear down your character no matter what you have done to help them and their families.

How you've dealt with men who disrespect you, mistreat you and expect you to forget it all in the name of "love".

How you've successfully raised a God-fearing young man without a father present. How you've dealt with the void of a man to guide him and how you've solely depended on me for help.

Stacie, stop discrediting what I have given you.

People are still trying to kill what I am trying to birth out of you. Abortion is not an option here. You are overdue! It's time to deliver. Get ready to PUSH!

You have endured enough pain; the labor phase should not last this long. It's Time!

You are ready, your body is ready and others are waiting to experience and receive what I have placed in you!"

Table of Contents

Foreword   4

Gods Promise   6

Introduction   8

The heart of the matter   10

Authors Reflection   44

Introduction

This journey called life is filled with ups and downs. There are good times, bad times, and sometimes sad times. You will have days filled with love, joy, and happiness.

There will be days you wished you had stayed in bed and days that you wish you were never born.

On the bad days, we all like to use the cliché "All of my good days out weigh my bad days..." and whether we want to admit it or not life will leave us with wounds.

I want to share my intimate conversations with God about some of life's wounds we experience and encourage and initiate the healing process.

"Today is your day! God designed this day to bring you closer to your destiny."

~Stacie Quotes

"Who says you can't have it all? Each day you have a new opportunity to own everything God desires for you. Joy, peace, love and prosperity. The choice is yours."

~Stacie Quotes

Psalm 139:14

NKJV

"I will praise You, for I am fearfully and wonderfully made; marvelous are Your works, and that my soul knows very well."

Father's Love...

A Father's Love is Correcting
A Father's Love is Forgiving
A Father's Love is Purpose-Driven
A Father's Love is Purposeful
A Father's Love keeps you focused and on track

Father, thank You for Your Love!
Your Love has kept me sane. When I was about to make insane decisions that would alter my entire life, Your Love saved me! You brought me back; you snapped my attention back to you! Thank You!

Father, Your Love brought me out of depression! I had lost focus, lost faith and, most importantly, lost me! Your Love held me! In spite of my stubbornness, my will to want my way; Your Love held tight, you didn't let go!

Father Your Love is Consistent, Persistent, Unwavering, Committed, and Strong!

Father, Your Love Always Conquers! Your Love Won me Back, Your Love fought for me when I couldn't fight, Your Love pushed me and made me walk when I was paralyzed in Fear!

Your Love rescued me from myself
You sent help when I didn't want it
You sent help when I didn't know I needed it
You sent help! Thank You!
Even when your help was rejected, you sent help, even when I ignored
you! You sent Help! Thank You!

How do I return this Love? How do I respond to this Love? How do I
keep this Love?

"Daughter it's quite simple and almost unbelievable.... All you have to do
is Serve Me"

"Obey My Word, it's your roadmap, your instruction."

Dear Heavenly Father,

I love you. Thank you for loving me, accepting me and keeping me. I am your daughter and that means the world to me to know whose I am. I will spend each day making you proud to call me Daughter!

"Don't waste your time, energy, and love on someone who doesn't receive or want it. You matter! Love Yourself"

~Stacie Quotes

Matthew 20:16

NKJV

"So the last will be first, and the first last, For many are called but few are chosen"

Are you qualified?

Are you qualified to handle me, A Real Woman of God?

Are you qualified to handle my anointing? Can you pray with me and for me? Can you pray for me even when I don't ask you to? Can you be my spiritual covering as God would have you to be? Can you encourage, support and have my back? Can you allow God to use me in ministry without being jealous?

Are you qualified to handle me emotionally? Will you give me a strong shoulder on those days when all I want to do is cry or will you walk away and leave me to cry alone?

Are you qualified to handle my intelligence? Will you be proud and amazed at my accomplishments? Will you encourage me to push harder to reach my destiny or will you discredit who I am, insult my intelligence and want me to "act dumb" when you are around?

Are you qualified to handle my heart? You see, God holds my heart it is valuable and precious to Him. He does not want His prize possession in the hands of "Unqualified people". Can you like me as your friend first? Can you love me unconditionally? Can you commit to fall in love with me daily? Can you tell me you love me without saying a word?

If you cannot meet these qualifications, then DO NOT APPLY, because I am only interested in QUALIFIED APPLICANTS!

Dear Father,

Thank you for keeping me! Thank you for keeping my heart and my mind. If it was up to me, I would not be selective

"Be mindful of who you allow in your inner circle, or who you allow to get close to you to learn your weakness"
~Stacie Quotes

Luke 8:15

NKJV

"But the ones that fell on the good ground are those who, having heard the word with a noble and a good heart, keep it and bear fruit with patience."

Be Patient

Ever wanted something so bad; so bad that you would do anything to get it? I can't figure out why I have desires in my heart and not have them fulfilled. I am not talking about lustful, sinful desires; I am talking about the desire to have a loving relationship, financial peace, debt freedom, mental peace.

Does God know that I am Lonely? Does God know that I am longing to be loved and to love? Does God know that I struggle to "make ends meet"? Does God know that some nights I literally cry myself to sleep only to wake up at 4:44am most mornings in a sheer panic?

I cry out to You daily, what do I do Lord?

God's Response:

"I will not let you down

All of your hopes and dreams are already fulfilled

I am waiting to Bless you with them

Please let me Bless you

Just put me first, I am not finished with you

I want to mold you into what I want you to be

Be Patient My Child."

"Learn to identify God's voice! Listen to His instruction and Move! He will give you strategies it's up to you to make it happen"

~Stacie Quotes

Psalm 139:14

14 I will praise You, for I am fearfully *and* wonderfully made;
Marvelous are Your works,
And *that* my soul knows very well.

Beautiful

You are Beautiful- Inside and out

I created you with detail and precision

You are made to be beautiful

Your beauty is seen even when you are not around

That's my design Daughter!

Wonderfully made to astound and astonish

Every aspect of your life is amazing!

Astounding Beauty, you cause others to wonder; "Who is she? How does she do it?"

Astonishing Beauty; your character, your personality, your integrity is beautiful.

What's so astonishing you say?

It's astonishing that through it all; The betrayal, the heartache, the disappointment, the many set-backs, the pain; You remain a BEAUTIFUL WOMAN OF GOD-Inside and out.

"Today everything you think, everything you do, everything you say and every step you take will be successful!"

~Stacie Quotes

Heavenly Father,
Your word says, "You shall also be [so beautiful and prosperous as to be thought of as] a crown of glory and honor in the hand of the Lord, and a royal diadem [exceedingly beautiful] in the hand of your God." (Isaiah 62:3 AMP)

If it's in your word it's TRUE! I am Beautiful! I am Beautiful! I am Beautiful! Help me to see my Beauty from within as you see me. Recognizing my inner Beauty builds confidence, and empowers me to accomplish anything! I will no longer speak against your word, from this day forth I only respond to BEAUTIFUL. In Jesus name. Amen

2 Corinthians 5:17

[17] Therefore, if anyone *is* in Christ, *he is* a new creation; old things have passed away; behold, all things have become new.

Bring something to the table besides your stomach

Children of God, you long for a Godly husband/wife. You say you want God to send you a man/woman who can support you emotionally, physically, spiritually, and financially. If these are the qualities you hope for in a mate, what do you have to offer?

Are you emotionally stable? Do you jump from relationship to relationship in fear of being alone?

Are you physically fit? I don't mean "Do you have the perfect body?" I mean do you eat right and exercise? If you are or have been sexually active, do you know your STD status?

Do you have a relationship with God? A lot of people think that just because they go to church every Sunday they are "spiritually fit". Do you spend time reading God's word? Do you talk to Him daily and allow Him to speak to you? Are you walking in the "purpose" God has designed for you?

Marriage is a ministry. You have to know who you are in Christ and what your purpose is before you join your "Ministry Partner"

How is your credit? Do you live paycheck to paycheck? Do you owe every loan company in town? Do you pay on one bill by sacrificing another? My child, please get it together!

God is not going to send you a mate for you to drag them down.

You have to know how to manage a household budget. If you are over 30 and still living at home or living "on" somebody else, what do you have to offer me?

Don't be a grown man/woman with nothing to show for the time you have been here.

Exodus 22:2

[2] If the thief is found breaking in, and he is struck so that he dies, *there shall be* no guilt for his bloodshed

Den of Thieves

These are people who allow the enemy to use them. They are sent on assignment to steal your Joy, Peace, Sanity, and Happiness.

They are jealous of you and your success and want to do any and everything to bring you down.

Who is in your den of thieves? You have to recognize who these people are and remember that they are on assignment.

Pray and ask God to show you Who They are. (List them)

When you recognize who they are, what their purpose is, you know what to pray for.

Give it to God immediately. You cannot fight this battle. God is the only one who will thwart their plans. When they see that every trap they have set for you didn't work, they will know that they are being used by satan, and they are wasting time by going against God's will.

Scripture Reference:

Isaiah 54:15 - If anyone does attack you, it will not be my doing; whoever attacks you will surrender to you.

God, I trust you! I will listen to you for guidance and instruction. You know what's best for me, who's best for me. I thank you for building my support system.

"Life has taught me that you can't expect people to be something or someone they are not capable of being (honest, dependable, truthful, a good friend). Free your mind and separate yourself!"

~Stacie Quotes

James 4:1

4 Where do wars and fights *come* from among you? Do *they* not *come* from your *desires for* pleasure that war in your members?

Let Go!

When you let go, you free yourself! You free yourself to love, receive, grow, and trust again.

Letting go means putting the past behind you, yes you were hurt, betrayed, heart broken, used, and mistreated.

One thing we must recognize is that none of this would have happened if YOU didn't allow it!

You opened yourself up to hurt, you allowed people in your "inner-circle" who do not belong.

Guard your heart, mind and body. You are precious and only a select few should have the privilege of getting close to you.

You do not have to be around people who mistreat you. Choose now to stay away from negative people.

If you continue to allow this negativity in your life you will never learn to Let Go!

If it's your family, love them from a distance

If it's your friends, pick new ones

If it's your co-workers, separate yourself from them

You will be better in the long run and others will see the change in your life

Keep bitter, scornful, negative thinking people out of your life. Don't allow your un-forgiveness to cause you to become a bitter, scornful, negative thinking person; you cannot be blessed if you are bitter, and scornful.

"Stop looking back, thinking back, and going back! Everything you desire in life is in front of you! Move forward!"

~Stacie Quotes

Matthew 11:28-30

[28] Come to Me, all *you* who labor and are heavy laden, and I will give you rest. [29] Take My yoke upon you and learn from Me, for I am gentle and lowly in heart, and you will find rest for your souls. [30] For My yoke *is* easy and My burden is light."

Release

It is time to let go!

"Let go of the hurt, betrayal, heartache, and bitterness.

I have called you to greatness Woman of God, and it is time you start walking in it!

Let go of those who mean you no good

Let go of those who misuse you, mistreat you, and talk you down.

Forgive, Forgive, Forgive!

"I cannot use you with the hatred and bitterness you have stored in your heart

Please allow me to heal your heart. I have been trying to for so long."

You have endured enough! It is REDEMPTION TIME!

"I am ready to give you everything you have been longing for.

Love, Acceptance, Respect and the Man of God to help carry you to your destiny

The time is now, move when I tell you to

Forgive when I tell you to, (remember how I have forgiven you)

When I show you something don't doubt that it is me.

I Love you, and honor your faithfulness to me.

Be strong woman of God, because your best days are on the way."

God,

"I declare that I will move forward! Doubt, Fear, and Forgiveness have been evicted. I will release so that I may receive!"

"Change is good! Embrace the change God brings to your life, Trust Him, He knows what's best for you"
(James 1:17)
~Stacie Quotes

John 3:16

[16] For God so loved the world that He gave His only begotten Son, that whoever believes in Him should not perish but have everlasting life.

So in love with you!

"I am so in Love with you, your heart can rest assure!

I Love you so much no one can take this joy

I Love you today, tomorrow, and forever more

My Love for you No Man will ever know

My Love for you can never fade away

This Love I have, you don't have to maintain

This Love for you will not leave you for another

This Love for you will not abuse, misuse, destroy or teardown

This Love I have will not be shared with another

Don't fret my beloved this Love is not one that you have to question

There is no doubt that this love is yours forever."

Father God,

I need an immediate open heart surgery. Remove all of the Doubt, Disappointment, Self-Hate, Bitterness, Hurt, Anger and Rage.

Cause my heart to connect to your heart. Cause my heart to desire your will for my life. Cause my heart to Trust You. Cause my heart to beat to the sound of your heart and form an everlasting Love connection. This is the safest Love Connection. I will forever love you God, because you first loved me. (John 4:19 Amp), in the matchless name of Jesus. Amen.

"This day was created with you in mind. It is filled with an endless supply of opportunity. Don't miss out! Grab hold! Stay focused!"

~Stacie Quotes

Isaiah 54:17

[17] No weapon formed against you shall prosper,
And every tongue *which* rises against you in judgment
You shall condemn.
This *is* the heritage of the servants of the LORD,
And their righteousness *is* from Me,"
Says the LORD.

When the weapons against you feel like they are prospering (Isaiah 54)

I know without a shadow of doubt that God's word says No Weapon formed against me shall prosper, but my friend how do you cope when it feels like everything is caving in on you?

What do you do when you have problem after problem with no end or relief in sight? It seems like the odds are against you. You can't get ahead and there is no one on your side. The strength you thought you had seemed to have diminished. It feels like you have not fight left.

You say: "God I serve you, I am faithful; I *think* I am listening to you and following your will, but all hell is breaking loose in my life. What do I do?"

"STAND UP ON MY WORD! You know that the weapons of warfare or not carnal. Your problems may be carnal, but you cannot attempt to fight with mere carnal solutions. The only way out is MY WORD"-Says God!

God's word says in Isaiah 62:4 "No longer will they call you deserted or name your land desolate. You will be restored both physically and spiritually."

You have gone through enough! I am here, says God. I am your covering. I will not cause your footing to move. I will continue to cover and protect you.

Gracious Father,

Please forgive me. I make a vow to you today to Trust you, Trust your way, and Trust your Word. I will no longer "take matters into my own hands". I know that I need you! I need your direction, your instruction, your guidance, and your protection.

Thank you for clarity to hear, see, feel, and know you! Amen

"For whatever is born of God overcomes the world and this is the victory that has overcome the world~our faith (1 John 5:4) No matter your situation today…You are victorious! NO THING, or NO ONE will stop what God has planned for you."

~Stacie Quotes

"God wants you to live a life of abundance! Guess What? YOU have to want it; to have it."

~Stacie Quotes

Matthew 18:22

[22] Jesus said to him, "I do not say to you, up to seven times, but up to seventy times seven.

When those you love betray you

What do you do when the people you look out for and give your very best betray you?

What do you do when the people you admire and rely on for guidance and direction betray you?

What do you do when the people you confide in betray you?

What do you do when your family betrays you?

STAND! Stand on God's Word. Know that God is molding you.

My child you are precious to me, I want you to have the very best. I did not bring you this far in life to leave you.

You need to know that you are being prepared. Preparation is ongoing! Nothing happens overnight, unless it is My Will. You must go through this process so that you will learn and apply what you have learned.

I want you to learn that you cannot trust everyone with your emotions. You cannot confide in man/woman and expect them to have your best interest in mind. Humans are very jealous creatures.

Listen to what they say to you, but most importantly watch how they act.

I have given you the gift of discernment, Use It!

God, help me to love past the hurt and confusion. Help me to remember You. My mind, my heart and my emotions are yours.

I will not allow my purpose and destiny to be blocked by an unforgiving spirit. I choose this day to apply Matthew 5:44, I will pray for those who despitefully use me. Amen.

"In the midst of confusion, chaos and hurt~ allow God to be your confidence, strong and firm"

~Stacie Quotes

"This is the Day! The day of Peace, Deliverance, Revelation, Love and Prosperity… Whatever you need, ~ today is Your Day to receive it! Why? Because this is the day that the Lord has made!"

~Stacie Quotes

2 Chronicles 8:16

[16] Now all the work of Solomon was well-ordered from the day of the foundation of the house of the LORD until it was finished. So the house of the LORD was completed.

Author's Reflection

Hallelujah! Thank you God for being the lover of my soul, for keeping me even when I resisted. Thank you for every heartache, every obstacle and every eye-opening life experience. I couldn't understand WHY at the time, but now I realize that I had to go through to publish my first book! You are a mighty, awesome, God and I will forever serve you.

There are so many people I have encountered over the years and it would take an entire book to thank you for how you contributed to my life. Some positive and some negative but I still say thank you because I am who I am today because of my life experiences.

To my son Cameron, raising you has been a gratifying experience. I am grateful God allowed me to teach, train, and help prepare you for adulthood. You are an amazing young man of God with a bright future ahead. Remain focused and let God lead you.

To my Spiritual Father-Pastor Lenny Gaines. Wow! You have taught me to use my Faith to get what I want. I stand today as a Confident, Strong, Powerful, Bold Woman of God, because of your teaching, instruction, guidance and correction. Thank you for being my confidant, father-figure and my Pastor!

To my natural parents, Patricia Earle, Harrison Thompson and Linda Thompson (step-mom). Thank you for raising a strong-willed little girl who's not afraid to take risks. You have always supported me on every endeavor without too many questions. You were always there to help with raising my son and I am forever grateful for the countless babysitting hours, and school pick-ups when I had to work late. You have always given me 100% of your time and love. Thank you.

My siblings: Maurice, Rashad, Tiffany, Robin, don't forget that I'm still the oldest! Keep striving for success. God has a plan already in place for you.

Malikah, Rayshad, Dontrell, Robin, Kavari, Jayden, Josiah, and Jada, if Aunt Stacie can publish a book you can do whatever you put your mind to. Dream Big and you will Live Big. Love you.

My PowerHouse Christian Church family thank you for the love, support and encouragement. To Joyce Hawkins, my spiritual mom, thank you for always being my voice of reason! You may not think so, but I appreciate and utilize every piece of advice and guidance that you give me.

My best friend Lisa, girl... thank you for all you have done. Over the past 23 years you have been my biggest supporter, my shoulder to cry on, an ear to "vent" to, my sounding board and my confidant. You are my "shero".

Chasity, aka "Little Stacie". I am honored that you look up to me as a mentor. You keep me accountable, and encourage me to make sure I am my best "Me" at all times.

Jessica, I am so glad God brought you into our lives. You are an amazing young woman of God and I look forward to watching you blossom into a wife, and mother.

To my sister, my friend, my road partner Calrinda... you have been my biggest cheerleader. Your sweet spirit always helps to keep me grounded. Thank you for always having my back. Love you girl!

To my friend Tyrone (Spank), your prayers and encouragement, motivate me to push forward. You are a great man of God who I am proud to call Friend.

There are several people I pattern myself after and look up to as a mentor. These people may not even know that I consider them as a mentor, but I would like to take the time to say thank you to the following people for their professionalism, integrity and character: Pat

Kelsaw, Byron Garrett, Edward Surratt, Caroline Caldwell and Gwendolyn Baker.

Finally to my publisher Marisa McClinton, thank you for believing in me and my writing. I am grateful for your professionalism and expertise; you have made it possible for me to present my first book to the world.

Author's Bio

Stacie Thompson, is an expert in the Youth Development/Community Outreach field. She has celebrated success with over 18 years of experience in her career field; as a former manager of grassroots mobilization for a policy and advocacy network, and former executive director for a community-based organization. Stacie earned a Bachelor's Degree in Psychology from Southern Wesleyan University and Masters of Science in Youth Development Leadership from Clemson University.

In addition to her professional duties and responsibilities, Stacie continues to mentor young men and women in her community. Stacie does not look at her career as "work" but knows that it is what God has called her to do in life. She is personally involved with the youth development and mentors the young adults she was previously acquainted with on a professional level. Her determination springs from an innate desire to please God. As a successful professional, Stacie strives to lead by example and show young adults that decisions you make today effect your tomorrow.

Anyone who knows me, knows that I Love butterflies! They symbolize my growth and maturity; physically, emotionally and spiritually.

Despite what it has been through, a butterfly is free, whole, beautiful, graceful and confident. I used the butterfly throughout my book as a reminder that no matter what comes my way, if I remain focused on God I will not look like what I have been through!

For more information or to schedule speaking engagements please contact:

Ms. Stacie Thompson

Spthompson71@gmail.com